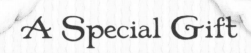

A Special Gift

For:

From:

Date:

A

Little

Book of

Blessings

Peace·Love·Hope·Health·Happiness

Illustrated by

DEBBIE MUMM

Brownlow

Little Treasures Mini Books

A Little Book of Blessings

A Little Book of Love

A Little Cup of Tea

A Roof With a View

Baby's First Little Book

Baby Oh Baby

Beside Still Waters

Catch of the Day

Dear Daughter ♥ Dear Teacher

Friends

For My Secret Pal

Grandmother

Grandmothers are for Loving

Happiness Is Homemade

How Does Your Garden Grow?

Mom, I Love You

My Sister, My Friend

Quiet Moments of Inspiration

Seasons of Friendship ♥ Sisters

Tea Time Friends

They Call It Golf

Blessed is this day.

It is the only day I've got.

May I use it wisely for

the things that truly matter.

-ANONYMOUS-

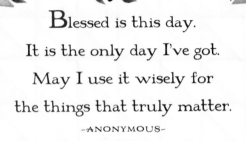

For everything you

have missed, you have gained

something else.

-RALPH WALDO EMERSON-

Come and see what God has done, how awesome his works in man's behalf!

PSALM 66:5

The word which God
has written on the brow
of every man is hope.

-VICTOR HUGO-

Remember the day's blessings;
forget the day's troubles.

-EARLY AMERICAN PROVERB-

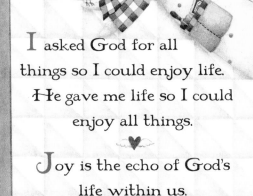

I asked God for all things so I could enjoy life. He gave me life so I could enjoy all things.

Joy is the echo of God's life within us.

-JOSEPH COLUMBA MARMION-

The more you give,
the more you get.
The more you laugh,
the less you fret.
The more you love,
the more you'll find
That life is good
and friends are kind.
For only what we give away
Enriches us from day to day.

God's gifts put man's best dreams to shame.

-ELIZABETH BARRETT BROWNING-

Whoever is happy will make others happy too.

-ANNE FRANK-

Happiness sneaks in through a door you didn't know you left open.

-JOHN BARRYMORE-

Peace to a Christian is not the absence of trouble, but the presence of God.

It is not what we
take up, but what we give up
that makes us rich.

-HENRY WARD BEECHER-

Reflect upon your present blessings,
of which every man has many —
not on your past misfortunes,
of which all men have some.

-CHARLES DICKENS-

May your
home be filled with peace,
And your heart with
hopeful cheer,
May your happiness increase
With each bright succeeding year.

—H. M. BURNSIDE—

I have learned to be content
whatever the circumstances.

—PHILIPPIANS 4:11—

The Lord gives his blessing

when he finds the vessel empty.

-THOMAS A KEMPIS-

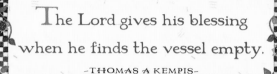

Serving God is doing good

to man.

-BENJAMIN FRANKLIN-

Kindness is one of the

most attractive assets of

the human race.

For attractive lips, speak words of kindness.

For beautiful eyes, look for the good in other people.

For poise, walk with the knowledge that you'll never walk alone.

Having some place
to go is home.
Having someone to love is family.
Having both is a blessing.

-ANONYMOUS-

Teach me, my God and King,

In all things Thee to see,

And what I do in anything,

To do it as for Thee.

-GEORGE HERBERT-

Whatever comes,
let's be content withall:
Among God's blessings there
is no one small.

—ROBERT HERRICK—

God has not called me to
be successful; he has called me
to be faithful.

—MOTHER TERESA—

He has achieved success
who has lived well, laughed
often, and loved much.
-BESSIE ANDERSON STANLEY-

You will seek me and find me
when you seek me with all your
heart. I will be found by you.
-JEREMIAH 29:13-

Every charitable act is a stepping
stone toward heaven.
-HENRY WARD BEECHER-

LOVE

Miracles

Heavenly Music
The Language of Angels

©DEBBIE MUMM

We are all strings in the concert of God's joy.

-JAKOB BOHME-

God's promises are like stars;
the darker the night
the brighter they shine.

-DAVID NICHOLS-

The means to gain happiness is
to throw out from oneself,
like a spider, in all directions an
adhesive web of love, and to catch
in it all that comes.

-LEO TOLSTOY-

I wish you all
the joy that you could wish.

-SHAKESPEARE-

Joy is that deep settled
confidence that God is in control
in every area of my life.

-PAUL SAILHAMER-

Those who bring sunshine to
the lives of others cannot keep
it from themselves

-JAMES M. BARRIE-

I asked for happiness for you
In all things great and small,
But that you'd know
His loving care
I prayed the most of all.

-UNKNOWN-

Praise be to the God and Father
of our Lord Jesus Christ,
who has blessed us in the
heavenly realms with every
spiritual blessing in Christ.

-EPHESIANS 1:3-

Peace·Love·Hope·Health·Happiness

MAY YOU HAVE

Enough happiness to keep you sweet;

Enough trials to keep you strong;

Enough sorrow to keep you human;

Enough hope to keep you happy;

Enough failure to keep you humble;

Enough success to keep you eager;

Enough friends to give you comfort;

Enough wealth to meet your needs;

Enough enthusiasm to look forward;

Enough faith to banish depression;

Enough determination to make each
day better than yesterday.

A person who is to be happy must actively enjoy his blessings.

-CICERO-

Glorious indeed is the world of God around us, but more glorious the world of God within us. There lies the land of song; there lies the poet's native land.

-HENRY WADSWORTH LONGFELLOW-

I said a prayer
for you today
And know God
must have heard;
I felt the answer
in my heart
Although He spoke
not a word.

God always gives his very best to those who leave the choice with him.

—JAMES HUDSON TAYLOR—

My God will meet all your needs according to his glorious riches in Christ Jesus.

—PHILIPPIANS 4:19—

If you are not satisfied with a little, you will not be satisfied with a lot.

Unwelcome visitors
sometimes bring
unexpected blessings.

-ANONYMOUS-

Not what we say about our blessings but how we use them is the true measure of our thanksgiving.

—W. T. PURKISER—

Each moment of time holds a gift in its hands.

—ANONYMOUS—

May the God of hope fill you with all joy and peace as you trust in him, so that you may overflow with hope.

—ROMANS 15:13—

He
who has
health,
has hope;
and he
who has
hope, has
every-
thing.

Bless our home,
Our lives, our friends,
With love, that Lord,
On Thee depends.

–ANTIQUE SAMPLER–

Every house where
love abides
And friendship is a guest,
Is surely home,
and home, sweet home
For there the heart can rest.

–HENRY VAN DYKE–

May the wings of love
enfold thee
Night and day;
May the strength of Love
uphold thee
All life's way.

–EUGENE S. FIELD–

The Lord bless you
and keep you;
The Lord make his face shine
upon you, and be
gracious to you;
the Lord turn
his face toward
you and give
you peace.

-NUMBERS 6:24-26-

May hope,
thy pilot
safely steer
Thee through all
dangers
far or near!

There is no medicine like hope, no incentive so great, and no tonic so powerful as the expectation of something better tomorrow.

– ORISON SWETT MARDEN –

May you be blessed by the Lord, the maker of heaven and earth.

– PSALM 115:15 –

Blessed are those who see
the hand of God in the
haphazard, inexplicable,
and seemingly senseless
circumstances of life.

–ERWIN W. LUTZER–

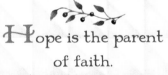

Hope is the parent
of faith.

–CYRUS AUGUSTUS BARTOL–

Count your blessings, name them
one by one!